THE MAGIC LANTERN
How Movies Got to Move

THE MAGIC

*by Judith Thurman
and Jonathan David*

LANTERN

How Movies Got to Move

Atheneum · New York · 1978

LIBRARY OF CONGRESS CATALOGING IN PUBLICATION DATA

Thurman, Judith   The magic lantern.

*   1. Moving-pictures—Juvenile literature.   I. David, Jonathan,*
joint author.   II. Title.
PN1994.5.T5   791.43'02   78-5197
ISBN 0-689-30628-8

Copyright © 1978 by Judith Thurman and Jonathan David
All rights reserved
Published simultaneously in Canada by McClelland & Stewart, Ltd.
Printed and bound by The Halliday Lithograph Corporation
West Hanover, Massachusetts
Designed by Mary M. Ahern
First Edition

for our fathers,
William A. Thurman and Jack David

Contents

THE MAGIC LANTERN
How Movies Got to Move

1 : The Acrobat

Why is there a small picture of an acrobat on every page of this book?

Flip all the pages quickly, and you'll find out.

All those separate pictures of the acrobat suddenly come to life . . . you see him move!

But what happens to the acrobat when you turn the pages slowly instead of flipping them?

The acrobat doesn't move at all. Each one of his pictures lies as flat and still as any other printed photograph.

What makes the acrobat move? Come to the movies and find out.

We've come into the movie near the end. It's a cowboy film—you know the one. The posse is riding out of town in a cloud of dust. The prospector's pretty daughter is standing guard at the mine. The outlaws are galloping across the mesa . . . while back at the saloon, Jake the bartender is polishing the glasses.

Now turn around and look behind you instead of at the screen. You will see, high above the seats, a little window with a strong light streaming from it. That's the projection room. Let's go up there.

The projector is a large, noisy machine. It has a pair of wheels that look like metal Mickey Mouse ears, turned sideways. In the top "ear" is the reel of film that is going to be shown. As the film runs through the projector, it is rewound in the bottom "ear."

The movie ends and the wheels stop. Let's take the film off the projector and look at it.

It's a long, thin strip of *celluloid*, which is a kind of plastic. One reel of film, if you unwound it, would stretch about a quarter of a mile! On the strip of celluloid are thousands of separate photographs. Each one is called a *frame*. Let's look at a short piece of the film closely.

At first all the pictures seem to be the same. Look again! There's a tiny difference between each one.

The projector of a big movie house ... the little window ... the metal "ears," open to show the reels of film.

This piece of film is from a cartoon. Cartoons are strips of drawings that have been photographed.

Here's the sheriff reaching for his gun. In the next picture he's still reaching, but his hand has moved a little. In the next picture, it has moved a little more. In the next picture he has just touched the handle.

When you saw the sheriff reach for his gun and draw, it happened—on the screen—in only a few seconds. It was almost too fast too see. But on the

strip of film, the sheriff's draw is a series of photographs, one for every split-second of his motion.

The projector flashes all these photographs on the
screen, one by one, very fast. When you flip the
pages of the book, you are also flashing photographs, one by one.

Moving pictures—movies or flip-books—are a
series of still photographs flashed at a certain speed.

But what makes them seem alive? Your own eye
does.

Your Persistent Eye

Look at this photograph of a man jumping a
hurdle. You can see every step he takes in his run
and jump. The photograph has stopped the movement, step by step, so you can get a good look
at it.

If you were watching the hurdler in real life, you
would be able to see him run and jump, but you
could never see his movement in such detail.

Why not?

The eye works very fast, but it still needs a little time to form each picture, and time for that picture to fade. So when many fast-moving pictures enter the eye, you can't see them all at the same time. It's as if each one has to wait its turn for your attention—though only for a fraction of a second.

Your eye may only be seeing picture **A** when the runner has already reached point **B**. Scientists call this holding action of the eye *persistence of vision.*

You can test your own *persistence of vision.* Try this:

Turn a bike upside down and spin the wheel. Do it slowly at first. When it spins slowly, you can see the spokes. Now spin it faster. When you spin it fast, you don't see separate spokes any more. Why? The pictures of the spokes in your eye have crowded together, overlapped, and so you see them as a blur of motion.

Hold a flashlight in front of you in the dark. Slowly move it in a circle. You can see the separate points of light as it moves. Now make a faster circle, faster! The points of light seem to "melt" together, to become a glowing ring. The eye can't see them separately any more. You know why: their pictures, too, have become a blur.

If this is true, why doesn't film, running fast through the projector, appear as a blur on the screen? It would—except for one thing. Between each picture and the next one there's an instant of darkness. Just for a fraction of a second, a *shutter* inside the projector shuts off the light between each frame. It is so short a time that you can't notice it. But it gives the eye just enough rest so that the pictures don't "melt" into a blur.

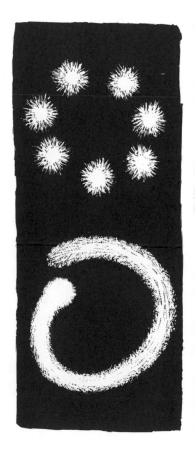

Why don't the pictures of the acrobat make a blur when you flip the pages? For the same reason. Your thumb holds onto each page just long enough so that there's an instant of darkness between the pictures.

Scientists call this "spacing" of the pictures by the shutter *intermittent motion.*

Your eye's *persistence of vision* . . . and the shutter's *intermittent motion* . . . makes it possible for you to see pictures move.

2 : Shadowplay

Have you ever watched a film or slide show in your classroom and then, when it was over, walked in front of the projector? The light of the projector throws your shadow onto the screen . . . your shadow pretends to choke itself, claws like a monster, steps on its own toe. And the class laughs! You give them a fine show.

Long before people could make movies, they used light, a screen, and shadows to tell wonderful stories that moved, with strange and funny characters.

This picture shows a scene that took place a hundred years ago, in Algeria. It gives you a feeling of what a shadow show was like. The audience gathered in the dark, as they do for movies. They waited, talked, ate snacks they brought. A small band played music to set the mood—and then the story appeared on the white screen.

If we could look behind the screen we would see how the shadows were made: by people hidden

above and below the stage, working *puppets* on sticks and strings, in the light of a fire.

Chinese magicians were the first to put shadows on a screen—a thousand years ago. The shows they gave were full of creatures like the Ox-headed Demon, the Monster-with-the-Many-Arms, and the White Serpent.

The magicians traveled all over China with their shows, reaching even the little villages. Their

A Chinese shadow puppet. The lacier the puppet, the more intricate his shadow.

screens were made of fine linen or paper. When the show was over, they could be rolled up. The flat puppets were cut out delicately from pieces of thin sheepskin and painted so that they glowed in color on the screen. Each puppet had several heads, which could be changed, so that with a small troupe of puppets, a wandering magician could tell many stories.

Musicians came with them, bringing their instruments—gongs, tambours and flutes. They played

during the shadow shows, and the eerie music helped, as it helps in the movies, to create suspense.

Shadow shows spread by caravan from China to almost every country of the Far East. In many places they were used as part of religious ceremonies.

Puppets like this one, from Java, danced at funerals. The audience treated the shadows with great respect, as if they were really spirits of the dead.

Here are *Karagoz*
and some friends . . .
Zenne, the maiden and
Beberuhi, the dwarf . . .

Celebi, a vain young
man, and Karagoz,
himself!

But in Turkey, people laughed and hissed and
booed at their shadow puppets. The Turkish
shadows clowned and romped on the screen the
way you did in front of the projector. The chief
puppet character was the loony *Karagoz*. The name
"Karagoz" means "Blackeye." And "Blackeye"
was, in a way, the grandfather of our modern
cartoon heroes: Bugs Bunny, Woody Woodpecker,
and Popeye. He, too, liked to beat people with a
bat, trick them, insult them, dump mud and
garbage on them. But he always took as many
tumbles as his victims.

Shadow plays reached Europe from Turkey about three hundred years ago. The king and queen of France watched them in their palace. Poor people gathered to watch them on street corners and in village squares. And in the big cities, special theaters were eventually built for the *shadows*. They were so popular in England, during the 18th century, that London, the capital, had at least four theaters, one with a screen fourteen feet high— as big as a modern movie screen.

These wooden shadow puppets, with their jointed limbs, danced for King Louis XVI of France and Queen Marie Antoinette.

In the nineteenth century, mechanical shadow puppets, made of metal, began to replace the older string or stick puppets which had been made from wood. Puppets like the huntsman on the next page, and the woodchoppers and their tree, were cut from zinc and tin and worked by wheels and pulleys beneath the stage.

Just as people like to show home movies today, people in the nineteenth century gave their own home shadow plays. They bought kits like the story of *Jack the Giant Killer*, complete with puppets, a stage and script.

The *shadows* were still lively only eighty years ago. And we would probably still be watching shadow shows if something better hadn't come along . . . the MOVIES.

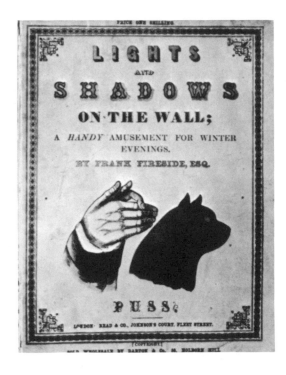

This shadow kit provided "handy" amusement for long winter evenings— shadow figures made with your hands!

Look out! A bat, a rat, and a horrible giant spider have all escaped from the soup tureen in this scene from a late 19th century shadow show.

These creepy creatures were designed by George MÉLIÈS (mel-YAY), a French shadow showman who also became one of the first movie-makers.

Méliès was the first to see the magical possibilities of the cinema, the first to film fairy tales and science fiction stories using special effects.

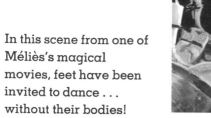

In this scene from one of Méliès's magical movies, feet have been invited to dance . . . without their bodies!

3 : Dark Rooms and Magic Lanterns

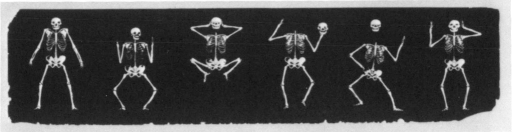

TWO RIDDLES:

> What weighs nothing, but can throw a house, a cow, or tree against the wall?
>
> How can a skeleton pass through a pinhole?

ANSWERS:

> *Light!* Light weighs nothing, but can throw—*project*—the picture of a house, or cow, or tree against the wall.
>
> A skeleton's picture can pass through a pinhole on a *light beam*.
>
> How? Wait.

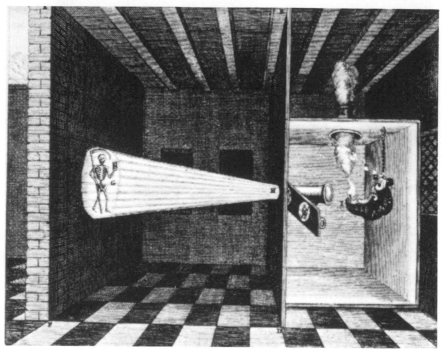

This skeleton has passed through a tiny hole . . . How?

On a light beam from the magic lantern.

About the time shadow shows came to Europe, a learned monk was trying to solve some of the riddles of light. He did all kinds of experiments with light. He bounced light off mirrors, tried to bend light with pieces of curved glass, studied how light and shadow worked in paintings to make them lifelike.

Then, using what he had learned, he invented something wonderful—a MAGIC LANTERN.

With this lantern the monk could throw pictures of a tree or cow onto a wall. He could make a

skeleton's picture pass through a pinhole on a light beam. And with the lantern he could show five or six colored pictures in a row and tell a story in changing scenes.

Projected pictures . . . changing scenes . . . was this a movie? No, none of the figures or scenes were real motion pictures.

What was this Magic Lantern? It was the first slide projector. Shall we go to the first slide show?

The learned monk, whose name was Father KIRCHER, gave the first magic lantern show for a small audience of priests and princes. The lantern

Father Athanasius KIRCHER (KEER-sher) (1601–1680), inventor of the magic lantern. Father Kircher was born in Germany, where he studied ancient languages and astronomy. While the Thirty Years' War was raging in his own country, he left to work in Rome. Rome was the home of many painters, inventors, and magicians as well as churchmen. The Romans loved magical entertainments, and Father Kircher probably went to see them, too. In 1646 Father Kircher published a famous book on light, *The Great Art of Light and Shadows*. "Light and shadows let us create all that is rare, marvelous and unknown in the world," he wrote. "So let us understand their power."

the mirror

the lens and slides

the picture!

the candle

amazed and even frightened them. To have a little fun, Father Kircher projected, among many other slides, a picture of the Devil. Some of the spectators, in their ignorance, thought the Devil was inside the lantern, making it work! Father Kircher probably explained to them:

"It's the power of light, not the Devil, that makes my lantern work. Come, look inside. There's no Devil here . . .

"The lantern is only this box, the size of a little room. There's no window—just this hole in one side . . .

"The light comes from the candle. I put a mirror behind the candle to bounce the candlelight toward the hole.

"Look closely. In the hole I have put a piece of curved glass. It's called a *lens*. Behind the lens I put the slide. No Devil's work—the slide is only a picture painted on a piece of glass . . .

"See! The candlelight bounces off the mirror and passes through the slide. The light beam picks up the slide's picture, then passes through the lens and out the hole! The lens points the light beam toward this wall outside. The beam carries the picture right over here, where I want it. There is no devil's magic in my lantern. I have made the light work for me."

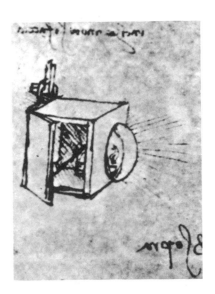

Two hundred years before Father Kircher arrived in Rome, the great Italian artist and inventor Leonardo da Vinci sketched his idea of a projecting ("bull's-eye") lantern. But he never built it. Father Kircher may have been helped by this sketch.

Light Works for Us, Too

Everything we see in the world is lighted for us in some way—by the sun, or by a lamp or fire. Light rays travel from these sources only in straight lines.

When these light rays hit something solid, like your brother, they bounce off in every direction. Millions of rays bounce off his nose, his toes, and everything in between.

Whatever the light has bounced off—that's the picture you see!

How do you see the picture? Your eye is designed to receive these rays of light, which form their

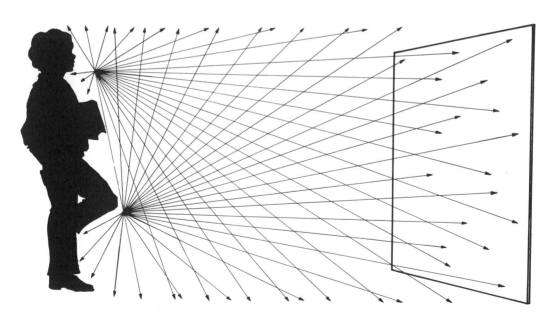

picture inside your eye as they did on the wall outside the magic lantern.

Your eye has a tiny opening which selects and limits the light rays that enter it—just as the lantern had its tiny hole. Only a narrow light beam can make a clear image. Too much light would cause a blur.

The tiny opening is called the *pupil*. When it is dark out, the pupil opens a little to admit more light. When it is sunny, the pupil closes a little.

Why does the light form its picture upside down in your eye? Track the path of the light rays bouncing off the boy, through the lens, onto the retina, and you will see what part of his picture lands where. But why would you see the boy right side up? Because your eye sends all its pictures to your brain via the optic nerve, and the brain reverses them for you.

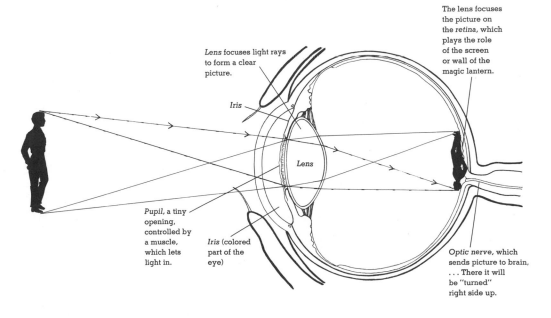

Lens focuses light rays to form a clear picture.

Iris

Lens

Pupil, a tiny opening, controlled by a muscle, which lets light in.

Iris (colored part of the eye)

The lens focuses the picture on the *retina*, which plays the role of the screen or wall of the magic lantern.

Optic nerve, which sends picture to brain, ... There it will be "turned" right side up.

Remember that the magic lantern had a lens in its hole? The eye has a lens, too. The lens gathers and *focuses* the light rays so that they form a clear picture.

So your eye and the magic lantern have basically the same parts. The lantern worked like your eye —only *backwards*. Your eye *receives* pictures on the light. The magic lantern *projected* pictures on the light.

The Lens

The lens in the magic lantern helped *focus* the projected picture. How did it work?

A man-made lens is a piece of thick, curved glass that has a special power to control and direct light rays. Many familiar things work because of lenses. A magnifying glass is a lens . . . so is a telescope. Eyeglasses have lenses . . . so do binoculars.

When a light beam enters the lens, the curve in its glass changes the beam's direction. The lens can *bend* light rays.

There are two kinds of lenses, and they bend light in two ways.

A lens that's *curved in* (concave) *spreads* the light rays apart.

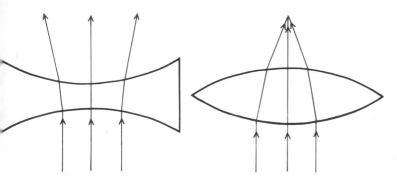

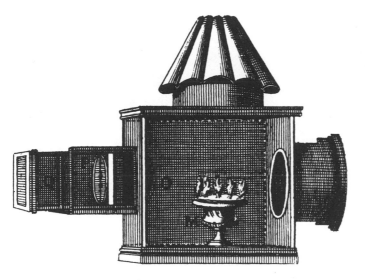

A careful sketch of a
small magic lantern.
The convex lens
is labeled "P."

A lens that's *curved* out (convex) bends the light rays together—toward one spot.

Because a convex lens bends the light together, it can *focus* a picture—make it sharper. Father Kircher wanted a sharp picture on the wall, so he used a convex lens in the magic lantern. He also wanted a right-side up picture. How could he get one? With an upside-down slide.

During Father Kircher's lifetime, the magic lan-

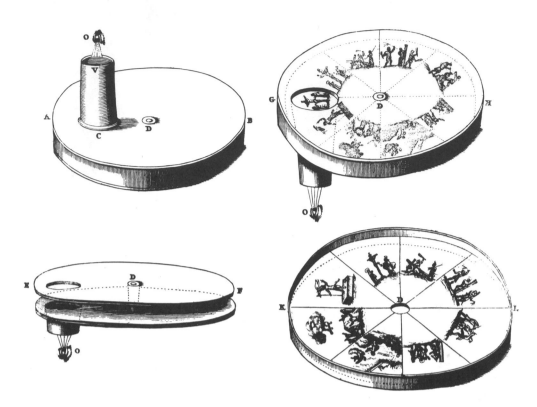

A drawing from Father Kircher's book, showing an idea for improving the magic lantern.

. . . Round discs that could be used instead of square slides. The discs have separate scenes painted on them. This idea of the discs was used centuries later— in a little different way —to project the first real moving pictures.

tern became as popular an entertainment as the shadow shows.

Other inventors began to improve the magic lantern and the art of projecting pictures. Father Kircher was not jealous—quite the opposite. "I could make many promises for my magic lantern," he wrote before he died in 1680. "But I shall leave those promises to the future."

These small, compact magic lanterns were designed by Johann ZAHN, the most famous of Father Kircher's followers. The little lanterns could sit on a table and be carried easily by one person.

This picture of a wandering magic lantern showman was etched two hundred years ago. You can see he has one of Zahn's little lanterns tied to his back. He and his lantern traveled from town to town in Italy and gave shows everywhere.

In this old etching, we see a magic lantern showman has a crowd spellbound on a Paris streetcorner.

The Great Lantern Horror Show

You're not afraid of ghosts, are you? You're not bothered by skeletons that slither through the air, or dead spirits wriggling up from dank tombs?

Good! Let's go to The Great Lantern Horror Show!

The year is 1798 and the horror show is about to take place.

It is billed as the *Phantasmagoria*, and it's the idea of a Belgian physicist who calls himself Robertson.

As a theater for his horror show, Robertson has rented a chapel outside Paris that is said to be haunted. The monks who once owned the chapel have decorated the walls with human bones!

Inside this house of bones, Robertson has built a small stage with a secret hiding place behind it for himself and his magic lantern.

His "horrors" are spooky slides shown by the magic lantern. But he has some special tricks that will terrify the audience.

Instead of projecting his slides onto a screen or wall, Robertson will make a screen of smoke, using herbs and chemicals. When the magic lantern flings its pictures onto the smoke, they'll shiver and flap and twist.

Now turn the page . . .

People enjoyed private
lantern shows, just as
later they had their
shadow kits, and later
still, home movies.
From this picture you
can see that the lantern
"showman" was
sometimes a
"show-woman."

To the audience, watching Robertson's *Phantasmagoria* in 1798, it seemed that these spectres had come from nowhere, had risen from the tombs in the chapel.

The skeletons seemed to rush at them... The demons twisted through space... The angels fluttered on the smoky air.

People fainted and fell off their chairs. And the *Phantasmagoria* made lots of money.

Robertson's *Phantasmagoria* was probably the grandest spectacle ever staged with a magic lantern.

Robertson's show had lots of copiers. This is a picture of a spooky show from the same era. Instead of using a slide, the lantern showman projects the figure of a live actress, with help from a big piece of sheet glass.

A few years later, when a new century began, a century of invention and technology, lantern shows became more educational and scientific.

One inventor found a way to convert an ordinary oil-burning table lamp into a magic lantern. He called it the *Lampascope*. It came with simple slides, which you can see on page 38.

Just as movies often take their plots from novels, magic lanterns showed scenes from books that were popular in the nineteenth century. On the next page is a dramatic moment from *Uncle Tom's Cabin*—the antislavery story written in America, just before the Civil War.

The Lampascope . . .
and three of its slides.

(1) Bargaining with the
Devil (2) Napoleon's
army retreating from
Moscow (3) Animals
boarding Noah's Ark.

The magic lantern gave curious people a glimpse of places they might never visit. This *panorama* of London was painted on a glass slide in painstaking detail.

People loved the lantern shows, just as they had loved the shadows. And they abandoned them only at the end of the nineteenth century, when the movies were invented. But unlike the shadows, the old lanterns lived on. They were the parents of a new kind of projector—a projector that also had a lens, a light, and pictures: the movie projector.

4 : Toys of Motion

So far, we have seen shadows that moved on a screen, and slides projected onto a wall. But none of these were real motion pictures.

Why not? Didn't the shadows move? Didn't the magic lantern make skeletons float through space? Couldn't it show a story in changing scenes?

Yes. But they were not separate pictures that the eye had to combine. Flip the book again. Remember what is happening to the pictures of the acrobat?

Separate pictures . . . rapid motion . . . and the eye. Those are the keys to making pictures move.

Early in the 1820s, a new kind of toy appeared in London toyshops—a little cardboard disc with a picture on both sides.

They were simple pictures—and there were only two of them. But they really moved!

The discs had a picture painted on their "heads" and a different one on their "tails."

The little cardboard discs on the facing page had a scientfiic name: *Thaumatropes* (THAW-ma-tropes)— which means "wonder-turners."

A bird . . . and a cage
A horse . . . and a rider
A bald man . . . and his wig.

By twirling the strings of the disc you made it spin, and once it was spinning fast enough, the bird went into his cage! The rider rode his horse! The bald man wore his wig!

The "wonder-disc" worked like the pages that you flip. When it spun, the eye formed a picture of the

Dr. Joseph PLATEAU of Belgium (1801–1883). As a boy, Plateau had wanted to be a painter, but his family forced him to study medicine. He brought his love of pictures to his scientific work—and was able to explain the eye's *persistence of vision*. But he had a tragic accident in the course of his work. During one of his experiments he had stared directly at the sun for twenty-five seconds. It damaged his eyes permanently, and in 1828, the same year he published his findings, he began to go blind. But even after he lost his sight, Dr. Plateau continued to experiment with light and motion—helped by students who described the results to him.

bird. Before the bird could fade, the eye formed a picture of the cage. It saw both pictures at the same time—a bird inside the cage.

The man who invented the discs, Dr. John Paris, knew that the secret of their motion was in the eye, and not in the pictures. He was aware of the *persistence of vision*, but he couldn't explain how it happened.

The man who *did* explain made movies possible. His name was Dr. Joseph PLATEAU (pla-toe), and he was a Belgian scientist.

The PHENAKITISCOPE.

By experimenting with his own eyes, Dr. Plateau was able to understand how all eyes see movement —how the images form, linger and fade. And he put his discoveries to work in a way people could enjoy—in a wonderful motion picture toy.

Dr. Plateau called his toy the PHENAKISTISCOPE (fen-a-KEES-ti-scope). That simply means "motion shower."

A series of movements, like the frog's hop, the bird's flight, or the spinning gear were carefully painted on the large pinwheels which you will find on page 46.

Each picture was separated by a *notch*. You held the pinwheel in front of a mirror, spun it, and looked at the moving pictures through the notches. You didn't see many, separate figures, but one figure, moving. The frog hopped ... the bird gracefully flew ... and the gear turned.

The notches, like the shutter in the projector, separated each picture so that they didn't streak together in a blur. The notches provided the *intermittent motion* between the moving pictures.

Now people had a magic lantern to project slides—and discs, pinwheels and drums that made pictures move.

Something important happened the day Baron Frans UCHATIUS (OO-KAH-tee-us) thought of putting the two together. He was able to project real movement on a screen!

On the next page is a picture of Baron Uchatius's special magic lantern, invented in 1853. Instead of a square slide, it had a glass disc with each step of a simple motion painted on it. It had a second, shutter-disc—shaped like a pie with one piece cut out. Wheels and pulleys turned both the picture-disc and the shutter-disc at the same time. And the

Baron Frans von UCHATIUS . . . and his magic lantern. The Baron was a general in the Austrian Army who spent most of his time inventing better guns. He believed the lantern could be useful for training soldiers, but his superiors did not want to try it.

lantern's light projected a simple moving picture through its lens, onto the screen—a horse that trotted!

Was this a movement projector? Yes! But it wasn't yet a movie projector. For one thing, the disc only had a few pictures, and the movement it could show was very crude. But more important, the pictures were not *real* . . . they were not *photographs* . . . they were only painted on glass.

There was still no way to show the movement of real people. There were no *movies* yet because you couldn't "take" a picture . . . you had to paint one.

What we had, now, was a moving picture projector. What we didn't have were real photographs to project.

A later model of the
lantern, with the
trotting horse lit up on
a screen.

The ZOETROPE was another moving picture toy based on *persistence of vision*. It was invented in 1837, by W. G. Horner. As you see, the Zoetrope was a slotted metal drum with a band of pictures inside. By spinning the drum and looking through the slots, you could see the acrobat juggling the ball with her feet.

Grownups loved Zoetropes and the other toys of motion as much as children. The Zoetrope the father is playing with, and the daughter is watching, is a fancier, late model. The moving pictures appear in the window of the cardboard frame. The cardboard is painted like a stage set —so the moving figures seem like actors on a stage.

5 : Photography: The Invented Eye

How did the man get upside down inside the box?

A camera took his picture.

Where's the camera?

The camera is the box!

Cameras without film have been used for centuries. At first they were simply small dark rooms. The word camera means "room" in Latin. The word for "dark" was obscura. So a dark-room camera was known as a CAMERA OBSCURA (ob-SKOO-ra).

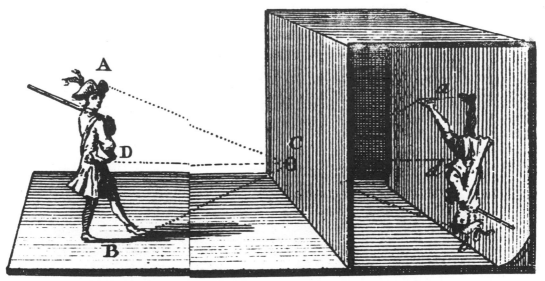

The camera *obscura* was a great help to painters, especially landscape painters. They carried their big box cameras around the countryside and set them up where they liked the view. Then they would cover the camera's picture with tracing paper and trace the outline of the scene. Later they painted in the colors. They were able to make extremely lifelike pictures this way.

Many of the inventors of photography had been part-time painters who worked from a camera *obscura*. The camera's picture was often so much better than their own that they tried to find a way of keeping it.

The camera *obscura* came in all shapes and sizes. Here we see what looks like a closet, but was really a portable chair camera. Next to it was a small "table model" camera with a tent.

Here is another big box camera. It has taken a picture of the house and trees.

These cameras are both three hundred years old. Even three hundred years ago you could take a real picture with a camera.

How do the cameras work? Just like your eye! Do you remember that your eye has a tiny opening, called the *pupil*, which limits the amount of light that can come in? The camera has a tiny opening like the *pupil*.

Do you remember how the narrow beam of light forms its picture, upside down, in your eye? Light forms its picture in the camera the same way.

This is a picture of a painter inside his *camera obscura*. It comes from Father Kircher's book, *The Great Art of Light and Shadows*. Father Kircher based his magic lantern on what he knew of these dark-room cameras. The magic lantern was a *camera obscura* that could project rather than receive light pictures.

A camera is a man-made eye. An eye is a natural camera.

Eyes and cameras can *take* pictures for you—but they can't *keep* them—not without help.

The eye sends its pictures to the brain, and the brain—your memory—stores the pictures, new ones and old ones. You can remember the way your teacher looked yesterday, but also the face of a friend from your old neighborhood, or how the yard looked when it snowed, or even the pony you glimpsed once from a car window.

Like your eye, a camera can't keep the pictures it takes—not by itself. A camera needs film. Film makes a print of the camera's pictures so you can always look at them again. Film is the camera's memory.

But three hundred years ago, there was no such thing as film. Even one hundred and fifty years ago, film had not yet been invented. The cameras we have seen could *receive* a picture, but not *keep* one. When you moved your big box camera, the picture was gone.

The Camera Gets a Memory

In the 1820s—about the time America was celebrating its fiftieth birthday—a Frenchman called Nicéphore NIEPCE (NEES-a-for nee-YEPS) was trying to make a camera that could print pictures, not just receive them.

Niepce knew that certain chemicals were sensitive to light: they turned black when the light hit them. He thought of coating a metal plate with the chemicals and leaving it inside his camera. He hoped that when the light entered the camera it would strike the chemicals and print a picture on the plate. He didn't expect a colored picture, just a pattern of black and white.

But the chemicals didn't work. So he kept rinsing his plate and starting over, trying some new mixture.

Then one day Niepce used a mixture of asphalt and varnish. As usual, he coated his plate, loaded his camera, and left it on the windowsill.

Nicéphore NIEPCE,

Did anything happen? Nothing seemed to. So Niepce, discouraged, went away.

But this time something *was* happening inside the camera. All day long, the light worked on the chemicals.

Niepce came home in the evening, eight hours later. When he opened the camera to clean the plate, he found a surprise ... a picture left by the light—the view from his windowsill! There were the rooftops of his neighbors' houses and even the scenery in the distance.

Niepce had taken the world's first *photograph*. And here it is:

It was a very exciting moment—but as you can see, it wasn't such an exciting picture. Now the problem was how to take a clearer photograph—and also take it faster. The rooftops could pose patiently for eight hours without moving, but could you?

While Niepce was struggling with his fuzzy picture, another man was working on the same problem. The other man happened to buy his materials

The view from Nicéphore Niepce's bedroom window, 1827.

from the same merchant Niepce used—and the merchant told him about Niepce's experiments.

The two men met, decided they would work as partners, and share everything they discovered. But Niepce died a few years later, before their work was made public, and the other man got most of the credit for inventing photography. His name was Louis DAGUERRE. (da-GAIR)

The Mirror With a Memory

Since it was not practical to wait eight hours for a picture, Louis Daguerre didn't wait. He took the metal plate out of his camera after ten minutes.

After ten minutes, there seemed to be nothing on the plate. But Daguerre found that when he steamed the blank plate with fumes of mercury, a hidden picture was revealed. The mercury fumes *developed* the picture that had formed after ten minutes. They made the light's invisible sketch strong and clear.

A photograph in ten minutes! A person would sit still that long. And Daguerre soon began taking pictures of people with his camera—mostly portraits of faces.

To make the portraits, Daguerre used a plate made out of shiny silver. When people saw their faces

appear on the silver plate, they felt they had looked into a mirror that held onto their reflection . . . a mirror with a memory.

It is always exciting to see a photograph of yourself. How exciting it must have been to see a photograph of yourself for the first time in history! Daguerre's pictures, which were called *Daguerreotypes* in his honor, delighted people all over Europe and America, and it was very fashionable to have your *Daguerreotype* taken.

Louis DAGUERRE, (1787-1851). Daguerre was a painter who had worked making scenery for the theater—big painted landscapes which he traced with the help of a *camera obscura*. It was hard work and took him many hours for every painting. Daguerre had often wished he could just take the picture in the camera home with him, instead of having to copy it, laboriously, himself. In 1829 he joined forces with Niepce, and ten years later, Daguerre announced to the world that he had found a practical way of making photographs.

Not all *Daguerreotypes* were pictures of people. This is one of the earliest ever made.

Look what was needed to take a *Daguerreotype* . . . practically a whole laboratory. For this reason, the pictures were very expensive, and only rich people could afford them.

Cartoonists poked fun at the photographers and their clients. These men won't spoil their pictures by wiggling— they're clamped to their chairs.

"You see, I place you first in my patent posing machine—that machine's quite an art in itself, too——."

"Then, by simply turning a handle or two, I screw you at once into a most natural and picturesque pose—quite an art. Put a little more contentment into the features, please."

Behold thy portrait—day by day
I've seen its features die;
First the moustache goes away,
Then the whiskers fly.

There was a problem with Daguerre's pictures. As the poem says, they faded! And once the Daguerreotypes faded, they were lost forever. There was no way to copy them. Each Daguerreotype was unique.

Because it was hard to smile steadily for ten minutes, most people came out looking serious, even a little grim, in their portraits.

Something had to be done to keep people's whiskers —and heads—from fading.

The Negative

The problem was solved by William Henry Fox TALBOT, an English inventor and part-time painter. Talbot invented the *negative*.

You have probably seen a negative. It is a piece of clear film with a picture on it. When you hold a negative up to the light, everything that ought to look black, is white. Everything that ought to look white, is black. White clouds in a dark sky look like black clouds in a white sky. White flowers on dark stems look like black flowers on white stems.

But this topsy-turvy picture acts as a *stencil* for the light. The light traces copies of the picture from the negative.

How? When you lay a negative over a piece of blank film, light will trace the picture onto it. But where the negative is black, it *blocks* the light . . . so the new picture there will be white. Where the negative is white, the light goes through . . . it turns the film black. So in those places the new picture will be black! All copies you make from a negative have the black and white in the right places.

Talbot had used tracing paper for his negative— there was still no such thing as clear, plastic film.

This is one of Talbot's
negatives . . . and its
copy . . . made around
1835.

The tracing paper had to be soaked in chemicals. Sometimes it got too wet—sometimes not wet enough—or there were uneven patches. And so the picture was often blotchy.

Another inventor, Frederick Scott ARCHER, found that a *glass* plate was better than the tracing paper. He dipped his glass plate twice in different chemi-

And this is Mr. William Henry Fox TALBOT (1800–1877) who invented the negative. Talbot had invented a practical process for taking pictures before Daguerre—but he had never published it. In the history of photography it is hard to decide who was really first, second or third with an invention. Many people—too many to name—often deserve credit.

Photographers traveled around the countryside with special dark-room tents, like this one, where they could develop their pictures on the spot. The little boy is the photographer's assistant. He is ready with the next plate.

cals—one coat for evenness, and one coat for sensitivity to light. Then he took his picture while the plate was still wet. This method gave him a fine and clear picture . . . in only a few seconds!

All these chemicals! Nitrates . . . iodine . . . acids . . . . . . salts . . . ethers . . . collodion . . . silver halides! You had to be a chemist to take photographs. And you had to work quickly . . . under a tent like this . . . in the dark. You had to coat your plate right on the spot, and take your picture fast—before the chemicals dried up.

Working under a tent was difficult and it wasn't healthy. A photographer who was also a doctor became very worried about the fumes he had to breathe. Dr. Richard Leach MADDOX realized that

what was needed was a simpler, safer, *dry-plate* for the camera. He tried mixing the chemicals with a gooey substance that would keep them fresh and sensitive to light—even after they dried. It worked! This magical goo was *gelatin*—plain, clear jelly made from soup bones. The *gelatin dry-plate* didn't spoil, didn't smell, and could be stored. It took a fine and even picture. And best of all, it took pictures much faster than the *wet-plate*.

The light worked on the dry-plate almost instantly —in ⅒th of a second. Later dry-plates worked in ⅟₅₀₀th of a second. That's faster than a human eye.

Niepce's camera had taken a picture in eight hours.

Daguerre's camera had taken a picture in ten minutes.

Archer's camera had taken a picture in a second or two.

But Dr. Maddox's camera could take your picture in a split-second. Even if you were laughing, waving, jumping—his photograph would catch you in the act.

But no matter how fast you could take a photograph, you could still capture only one frozen moment at a time. There could be no movement within the borders of a photograph. There could be no change. To see and record movement, you have to be able to keep on taking pictures—dozens of pictures, hundreds . . . thousands. Our eyes can do that. But no camera could—not yet.

6 : Bodies in Motion

Two men stood by the rail of a racetrack arguing about a horse. Was there a moment when that racehorse, trotting around the track, had all four legs off the ground at once?

Yes, said one man—Governor Leland Stanford of California, who owned horses.

No, said his friend—Freddy MacCrellish, who owned horses too.

The grooms and jockeys couldn't help them, and neither man could convince the other. They needed a picture—a picture of the horse in motion.

This argument took place a hundred years ago, about the time dry-plates were invented, but before anyone had ever taken a photo of an animal in motion.

Stanford went to an English photographer named Edweard MUYBRIDGE (Edward MY-bridge) to ask if he would try to take such a picture. Muybridge was interested in the problem. He agreed to try.

It was clear to Muybridge that he would have to photograph each instant of the horse's movement— not all the way around the track, but at least for a little stretch. He could not follow the horse with one camera. So he would need several cameras! This meant his timing would have to be exact. And the stage for the pictures would have to be set very carefully.

Edweard MUYBRIDGE (1830–1904), the first man to capture motion in photographs, was born in England to a poor family and came to America to seek his fortune. He went West like so many other ambitious men, taking pictures of the landscape, of American Indians, and of the cities he stopped at on the way. In 1875, Muybridge was accused of killing a man who had loved Mrs. Muybridge—but the jury acquitted him. After the scandal and the trial, Muybridge continued to work with Stanford on his motion photos, which finally brought him the fame that he had sought.

A view of Muybridge's setup for taking motion photographs.

The wall . . . helpers making measurements . . . the track . . . and the camera shed.

A horse beginning its run past the twenty-two cameras in the shed.

Stanford was a rich man and willing to provide whatever Muybridge needed.

First they built a special racetrack, covered in rubber to damp down the dust. On one side of the track they built a shed forty feet long. On the other side a high white wall. The wall was like a screen, a backdrop for the pictures. The horse they chose was Occident, whose glossy black coat would show up well when he passed in front of the white wall.

Muybridge then set up twelve cameras inside the shed—one every three feet. He strung a wire from each camera across the track. The cameras were rigged to go off one at a time—like a row of falling dominoes.

On a day when the light was good, and the track and cameras were ready, Stanford gave the signal. Occident trotted down the track. His hooves tripped the wires, and the cameras clicked.

What did the pictures look like?

What do these pictures show us? A complete movement in separate photographs—the key to moving pictures.

Muybridge went on to study many other motions with a row of cameras. Sometimes he used twenty cameras . . . sometimes he used forty!

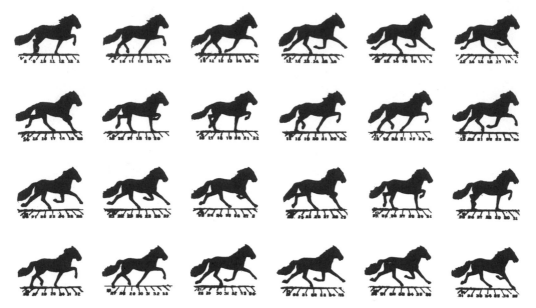

Occident trotting, 1877.
If you look closely, you
can see who was right
about the horse's legs!

Muybridge's pictures
of a jumping cat . . .

Do you recognize our acrobat? He was one of Edweard Muybridge's subjects.

Motion photographs like these made Muybridge famous. He published them in a book and traveled

A galloping camel.

Both series were taken with twenty cameras.

all over the country, lecturing on the art of capturing motion with a camera.

People had never seen a horse's gait in such clear steps before. Some of the steps looked strange to them. They didn't believe the pictures were true to life.

How could Muybridge prove his photographs were exact? He could project them! And so he did, using a special magic lantern called the *zoopraxiscope* (zoo-oh-PRAX-a-scope, "animal motion machine"). The horse, Occident, then trotted across the screen and seemed so real, wrote one reporter, "that all that was missing was the sound of hooves."

Had Muybridge invented movies?

Not yet. Not quite.

This is the magic lantern Muybridge used to project his pictures. It was called the zoopraxiscope. It had revolving discs, like the pinwheels Dr. Plateau designed. The discs (bottom) look a little like 45 rpm records.

7 : The Camera Rolls

We are still not ready to go to the movies—not while it takes forty cameras to photograph one action!

Even though Muybridge could project his pictures with a magic lantern, there were only enough pictures for a half-second of movement. Today, a thirty-second commercial on television uses about seven hundred separate pictures. A two-hour movie uses about one hundred seventy thousand separate pictures. How do we photograph so much action, take so many pictures? Not with seven hundred cameras, or with one hundred, seventy thousand separate cameras . . . but with one camera. A *movie* camera.

What's special about a *movie* camera? What makes it different from a *still* camera?

In any camera, a shutter guards the little opening where the light comes in. The shutter is like an eyelid. It opens to let the light in, but only for the fraction of a second needed to make a picture.

The shutter's quick opening and closing is like the blink of an eye.

A *still* camera can blink once—to take one picture. Then you have to turn the film and press a button to take another picture.

But a *movie* camera can keep blinking. It has an automatic shutter that opens and closes twenty-four times every second, or more. It takes twenty-four separate pictures in that one second. And you don't have to turn the film before every new picture. The film—a long strip on a metal reel—un-

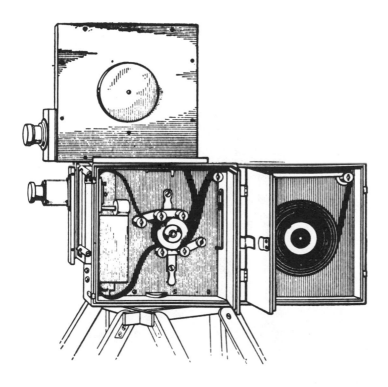

An old-fashioned movie camera, open to show how the reel of film unwinds. The unexposed film is in the top box. It passes in front of the shutter, and is rewound on the back reel.

winds automatically. The film keeps moving and the shutter keeps blinking until you stop the camera or finish the reel.

The Photo-Gun

Today we speak of *shooting* a movie. Well the first camera that could blink more than once *did* shoot its pictures. It looked like a gun . . . you aimed it at your subject . . . and pulled a trigger!

The Photo-Gun in action.

A picture of a bird in flight taken with Dr. Marey's Photo-Gun.

The Photo-Gun was invented by a French doctor named Etienne MAREY (ma-RAY) (1830–1904). Marey had studied motion for many years, using a gadget he attached to the hooves of animals. After he saw Muybridge's motion photographs he, too, began working with a camera.

But Marey wanted a simpler way of taking motion photographs than with the row of cameras Muybridge had used. You couldn't take twelve cameras into the woods to study birds, or to the aquarium to study fish. And they were very expensive too. So Marey designed *one* camera that could take twelve pictures at a time.

Inside the Photo-Gun you can see the parts of its camera . . . The opening and shutter . . . the glass dry-plate (the tiny squares are the coated parts of the plate) . . . And the lens.

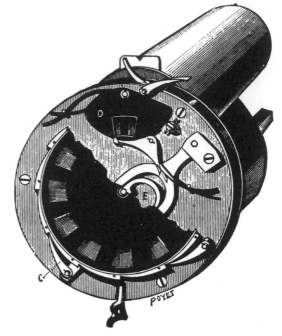

Even close up, the Photo-Gun looks like a shotgun.

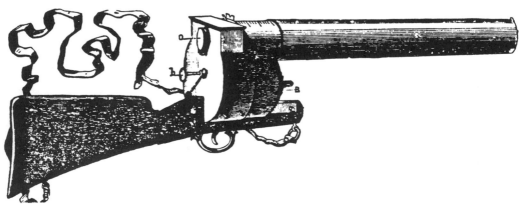

This is the Photo-Gun. It took its pictures on a single round glass dry-plate, that turned when you pulled the trigger.

Dr. Marey aimed his Photo-Gun at a moving animal, like this bird in flight. He pulled the trigger, the glass plate turned, the shutter blinked twelve

times, and the camera "shot" twelve pictures of the bird on the rim of the plate.

But the Photo-Gun still wasn't a movie camera.

The trouble was its glass dry-plate. It could only take a certain fixed number of pictures—never enough to make a movie.

So the glass plate had to go.

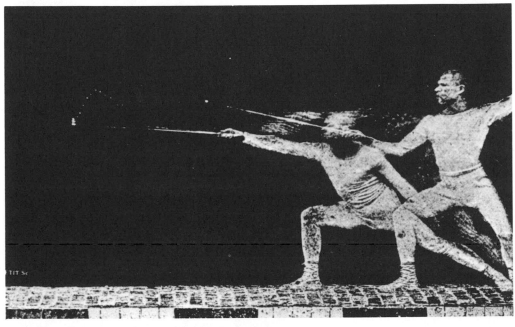

Marey took this picture of a fencer with *one* dry-plate, but the camera he used had a shutter able to blink many times. He called this a "Time-Picture" (chronophotograph). It looks a little like a slow-motion shot in a movie.

An early box camera,
one of the first to
use roll film.

About this time (the 1880s), an American inventor
named George EASTMAN thought of making dry-
plates for a camera out of paper. He coated a long,
thin strip of paper with a gelatin-and-chemical
mixture, and when the paper dried, he rolled it up
into a small cylinder. This cylinder was the first
roll film—and it was so simple to use and so light
to carry that it made it possible for anyone to use a
camera.

At first Edison used his
movie camera to make
peepshow films. The
"peeper" was a wooden
stand with a glass
window. You looked
into the window and
saw a very tiny, very
short moving picture.
On the next page is a
scene in a peepshow
parlor.

Eastman founded a company called KODAK to
manufacture a small box camera for his new film.

The Kodak camera was not a movie camera—
but it was the first camera to use roll film. People
all over the world bought Kodaks and rolls of film,
and snapped millions of pictures of each other.

A few years later, paper film was replaced by
something much better: *celluloid*, a kind of plastic.

Celluloid was sturdier than paper, and it didn't burn or snap easily.

Wouldn't a long roll of celluloid be just the thing for a movie camera!

Several inventors had the same idea at once: put a roll of celluloid film in a camera with a shutter that kept blinking . . . Find a way to make the film unwind automatically inside the camera . . . And then take motion pictures!

The peepshow machine, like so many "toys" of motion, had a fancy name: *Kinetoscope*. That just means "motion shower." Edison sold his "peepers" to a showman from New York, who opened a peepshow parlor on Broadway, in 1894. Here you see some elegant people peeping.

There were at least three models of the movie camera produced within a few years of each other. There was one in France, one in England, and one in America, it was made by Thomas EDISON.

Edison had already invented the light bulb and the phonograph. Now he was interested in motion pictures. Partly because he had the best laboratory, the most money, and excellent helpers, Edison was able to perfect his camera first—by 1894.

Could Edison take motion pictures with his camera?

Yes! Forty-eight pictures every second.

Did he use the camera to make movies?

Not right away. He decided movies didn't have any future.

8 : The Light Brothers Present ... "Baby's Breakfast" (Rated G)

We now have a movie camera—it is much faster than our eye and can stop motion many times a second. We now have film—a long ribbon of celluloid that records the pictures. And our persistent eyes are ready to combine the pictures and see the motion.

What's missing?

So far, no one has projected these celluloid pictures onto a screen.

Lots of pictures and photographs have been projected by various models of the magic lantern. These pictures even seemed to move on a screen— but only for a second or two.

Just as you couldn't photograph motion efficiently without film in your camera, you couldn't *show* motion efficiently without a projector built to handle the film.

As in the whole history of moving picture inventions, there were many people who were *almost* first with a projector. People built on and borrowed from and even stole each other's ideas.

But the credit for the first working projector goes to two French brothers who owned a film factory in Lyon, France. They were Louis and Auguste LUMIÈRE (loom-YAIR). The name "lumière" means "light" in French. So it turned out that the "Light Brothers" made the world's first movie!

Based on what they knew about Edison's camera, the Lumière brothers made one of their own.

Based on what they knew about the magic lantern, and its latest models, they built a projector. It had light and lenses, and it could unwind rolls of celluloid at the right speed. There was a shutter to provide the instant of darkness needed between each picture.

Film was not a problem for the Lumières, since they owned a film factory. But they had to order the plain celluloid from Eastman. When it came, they coated it themselves.

And then they made a movie.

Louis and Auguste
LUMIÈRE . . . from a
poster advertising their
movie house.

What do you think the first movie was? A spy
thriller? A gangster story? A Western? A ro-
mance? A horror film?

The first movie showed a baby girl eating her
breakfast. It was called "Baby's Breakfast."

Shall we go to the sneak preview? A few friends
have gathered at the Lumière's laboratory. There's
a small screen, no bigger than a home movie screen.
We sit back in our chairs to watch the first and
only scene of "Baby's Breakfast." There are only

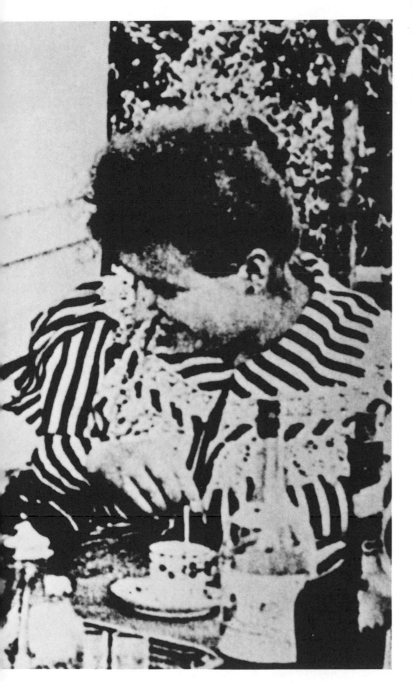

"Baby's Breakfast."
The baby was really
the daughter of
Auguste Lumière
and his wife.

A poster for the Lumieres' films playing in London.

three characters—Mama, Papa, and Baby. Their movements are jerky. Papa feeds Baby. Mama wipes her chin. The grainy film has scratches on it. The light flickers. Baby takes a few spoonfuls of her cereal, and in a minute the movie is over. But everyone heartily applauds.

Soon the people of Paris could go to the movies. Louis and Auguste opened the world's first movie house on December 28, 1895. Admission was one *franc* (about twenty cents).

And that was less than a hundred years ago.

The Lumières's
projector.

A famous poster
advertising the
Lumières' movie house,
called, in French, the
Cinematographe
(SIN-a-mat-o-graf).

This was a scene from one of the Lumières' first films—"Women Workers Leaving the Factory." The Lumière brothers used their camera to catch ordinary people in the daily movements of their lives.

Another early Lumière film. The scene shows people playing backgammon.

Edison's first film studio in New Jersey.

Edison changed his mind about the future of movies and went back to work on a projector. He built one a year after the Lumières, and he called it the *Vitascope*. This was an advertisement for the *Vitascope*, which showed how it could be used.

Making a movie in
America, around 1900.

9 : Coming Attractions

How long had it taken movies to begin moving?

If we start counting from the first shadow show—a thousand years!

Five hundred years to work on the camera, to capture the first picture, to make the first photo-series of a motion.

Centuries to develop the magic lantern, to play with motion, and finally to project moving pictures on the screen.

A lifetime to improve film—from a metal plate, waiting on a windowsill for its picture, to a strip of plastic, rolled on a reel, that can take pictures instantly.

But almost as soon as the Lumières showed their first films to the public, movies began to move everywhere.

"Baby" Lumière, of "Baby's Breakfast," is just the same age as the movies. Let's see what happens to the movies in her lifetime.

When she is a year old, Edison opens the first movie theater in America. He has decided movies will be popular after all! In a studio in New Jersey, he begins making films.

When "Baby" is a toddler, movie houses spring up everywhere. They have fancy fronts and fancy names—The Biograaph, The Palace, The Palladium.

While she is cutting her first permanent tooth, older children in America are going to Saturday matinees. A ticket for the "pictures" is usually a nickel, but on Saturdays, two can get in for the price of one . . . so does anyone have three cents?

The movies the children watched on Saturdays had come a long way since "Baby" made her debut. They had lots of action. There were villains in capes and moustaches, who tied heroines to the railroad tracks—heroes rescued them just in time! There were funny policemen with fat faces, who chased their crooks and each other in old jalopies.

There were faithful dogs who rescued their masters from danger, and outlaws who rode across mesas, and bartenders who polished glasses.

Every movie house had its piano player, pounding out suspenseful music. For on the screen, no one ever spoke a word, or made a sound. These were the *silent pictures*.

When "Baby" Lumière entered her teens, a place called Hollywood began to grow along with the palm trees in a sleepy suburb outside Los Angeles.

If she had been able to hang pictures of movie stars in her room as a young woman, they would have been pictures of Douglas Fairbanks and Valentino, of Mary Pickford and the great comedian, Charlie Chaplin.

What happens to the movies when "Baby" grows up? The movies grow up too...they begin to talk!

Baby has talked since she was two or three—the movies learn to talk at the ripe old age of thirty. But once they can talk, their sound becomes just as lifelike as their movement. From *movies* to *talkies* in only thirty years.

What does Baby Lumière do with her youth? Perhaps she travels and sees the world, falls in love, and has adventures. She certainly lives through the Great Depression. And so do the movies.

It is a bleak time in the world, but not on the screen. By the 1930s, movies (also in their thirties) are full of *color*.

When Baby Lumière and the movies both celebrate their fiftieth birthday, a new kind of moving picture is waiting in the wings...TELEVISION. But that is another story.

There is a good chance that "Baby" Lumière is still alive and over eighty. Perhaps she has great-grandchildren your age. If so, they love to hear the story of how she starred in the world's first movie. "Movies are only as old as I am," she might tell them. "Who knows what will happen to them in *your* lifetimes?"

"I make no promises for my magic lantern" said *Father Kircher, and he was a wise man. "I leave those promises to the future."*

The authors wish to thank the following for permission to use photographs and prints:

The following pictures are used Courtesy The Museum of Modern Art/Film Still Archives: pictures on pages 18 bottom, 64, 85, 86, 89, 93 bottom, and 94.

Thames and Hudson Limited, publishers of *The Archaeology of the Cinema* by C. W. Ceram for the use of pictures from that book.

The Gernsheim Collection, Humanities Research Center, The University of Texas at Austin for the pictures on pages 3, 6-7, 40-41, 56, 57, 61, 62, 66, 67, 68, 71, 80 bottom, 81, 83, and 84.

The Kodak Museum, Rochester, New York, for the photograph on page 65.

791.43 Thurman, Judith
THU
        The magic lantern

DE17'80	DATE		